Samuel Ireland

Mr. Ireland's Vindication of His Conduct

Respecting the publication of the supposed Shakspeare mss.: being a

preface or introduction to a reply to the critical labors of Mr. Malone in his

Enquiry into the authenticity of certain papers, &c., &c

Samuel Ireland

Mr. Ireland's Vindication of His Conduct
Respecting the publication of the supposed Shakspeare mss.: being a preface or introduction to a reply to the critical labors of Mr. Malone in his Enquiry into the authenticity of certain papers, &c., &c

ISBN/EAN: 9783337323165

Printed in Europe, USA, Canada, Australia, Japan

Cover: Foto ©Thomas Meinert / pixelio.de

More available books at **www.hansebooks.com**

Mr. IRELAND's
Vindication of his Conduct,

RESPECTING

THE PUBLICATION

OF THE

Suppofed Shakfpeare MSS.

BEING

A PREFACE OR INTRODUCTION

TO

A REPLY

TO THE CRITICAL LABORS OF

Mr. MALONE,

IN HIS

" ENQUIRY INTO THE AUTHENTICITY OF
" CERTAIN PAPERS, &c. &c."

LONDON:

PUBLISHED BY MR. FAULDER AND MR. ROBSON, NEW
BOND STREET; MR. EGERTON, WHITEHALL;
AND MESSRS. WHITE, FLEET STREET.

1796.

(iii)

ADVERTISEMENT.

THE following sheets originally formed a part of a work now in confiderable forwardnefs, as a reply to Mr. Malone's critical labors on the fubject of the Shakfpeare MSS. The body of this work required confiderable refearch, and, fo large a portion of time for its completion, as to render fome further delay unavoidable in the publication of the whole. But this part of the work having been completed and ready for the public eye, I have yielded to the importunities of my friends, who have fuggefted to me the neceffity at this moment, of laying before the public fuch further particulars as relate to my conduct therein. It will be obferved that I have adverted in the courfe of the following pages to Mr. Malone: and if the animadverfions fhould be deemed irrelevant, I truft, that no other apology is neceffary, than the intimation already given, of my having intended this Vindication as an introduction to the work alluded to, and therefore that it was a more eligible plan, not to make any deviation from the method, I at firft determined upon purfuing.

A recent circumftance, with which the Public is well acquainted, feems to call for this Vindication, and
even

even (painful as it is) to impofe the meafure upon me as a folemn duty, and obligation. I allude to the public ftatement, made by my Son. The world to which he has appealed, will judge and pronounce upon the truth of the allegations, and the weight of the teftimonies, which he has laid before them. I beg to affure the public that the refutation of Mr. Malone's book fhall be brought forward with all poffible fpeed; in which, whether the papers imputed to Shakfpeare are genuine or not, it will be clearly fhewn, that he embarked in this enquiry as utterly deftitute of the information of a philologift, and the acumen of a Critic; as it will, by his grofs and repeated perfonalities, be manifefted, that his felfifh and interefted views have made him throughout lofe fight of the manners of a Gentleman.

ERRATA.

Page 12, laft line but 1, after *my* read *friends*
12, line 10, after *to* add *the*
18, — 11, for *it* read *them*
27, — 13, before *Frank* read *John*
30, — 1, for *enter into* read *make*

A VIN-

A

VINDICATION, &c.

THE moſt unequivocal charaċteriſtic of an enlightened age, is the licence which is indulged to all, of free communication with the public on doubtful, and controverted ſubjeċts. There are, indeed, ſome queſtions, in the diſcuſſion of which it will be always difficult to perſuade the world, that mutual toleration is the moſt conducive to the intereſts of truth, and the moſt auxiliary to the operation of human reaſon.

But on topics of merely literary reference, that theſe enmities ſhould at all exiſt, muſt appear ſingular, and even paradoxical. For in literary conteſts there is ſcarcely any appeal to any

A   paſſion.

paffion. They can neither provoke the hopes, nor vibrate on the fears of mankind, to any confiderable degree. It muft, therefore, be a fatisfactory reflection to thofe, who have remarked on the hiftory of the human mind, that the mutual hoftility, and bigotry, which once deformed the writings of critics and philologifts, is at this moment, with few exceptions, totally extinguifhed. Pofterity, when they read the works of Salmafius, or Bentley, will be perplexed, even in finding motives for a fpirit fo intolerant, and a zeal fo intractable on matters of fuch light, and trivial import.

There are, however, exceptions to a remark, fo honorable to the tafte, and liberality of our age. There are ftill fome remnants of that *exploded difcipline*, which from the difufe into which it has fallen, muft at this time, be highly difgufting to the lovers of Englifh literature. The arrogance of fchoolmen without their learning, the rancour of controverfy without the wit by which it is embellifhed, muft at the prefent period, demand the severest, and most exemplary animadversion.

Mr. Malone has acquired, it may be said, some degree of literary reputation. It is that sort of reputation, to which a laborious and patient frame of mind, in all the departments of literature has its peculiar pretensions. But neither Mr. Malone, nor any other labourer of the same description, has any privilege of over leaping the province, to the drudgery of which a limited capacity has destined him, while a patient, and charitable world does not deny him the small pittance of fame, that arises out of it. *Illâ se jactet in aulâ.* Mr. Malone, of all writers, has the slightest pretensions to that majesterial character, he has lately assumed, and by virtue of which he undertakes not only to discuss, but to decide on literary questions, as well as to asperse the moral reputations of those, who differ from him in opinion.

The appeal, which I am now about to make

from the fentence, which this gentleman has paffed upon the papers in queftion, primarily origi-
nates from that folicitude to vindicate my own
character, which it muft be naturally fuppofed,
I cannot but feel on this occafion. Whether the
critical reafonings of Mr. Malone are folid, or
unfounded, whether he is entitled to any degree
of reputation, as a philologift, or critic, by the
publication of his enquiry, are queftions of which
the difcuffion will be poftponed, till my anfwer
appears before the public. At prefent I am
merely claiming the attention of the reader to
thofe topics, which relate to my own perfonal
agency in the tranfaction.

With regard to the manner in which my
own character is attacked, it will unqueftionably
be expected that I fhould fpeak fully and amply.
It is true Mr. Malone deals only in infinuations;
and infinuations, malevolent and flanderous as
they are, may eafily be repelled. It is true alfo,
that thefe infinuations are conveyed in a manner,
which neither refembles the overbearing acute-
nefs

nefs of Dr. Bentley, nor the fubtle poignancy of Bifhop Warburton. But infinuations may be troublefome, and even noxious; becaufe the dulleft being alive may at length, by reiteration and importunity, in fome meafure, atone for the bluntnefs and impotence of the fhafts with which he affails you. It may indeed be faid that thefe attacks are of a puny and ineffectual nature, but to remain indifferent to fuch attacks, is a philo-fophy which I have never arrogated; and it would look like a fort of affected ftoicifm, to appear filent and unmoved, amidft fuch mali-cious and calumniating afperfions.

Through the whole courfe of his pamphlet, Mr. Malone fpeaks of the " Impoftor," and the " Impofture." I remember in Mr. Locke, a long chapter on words, and the intellectual affocia-tions which belong to them. In a well-known effay on the fublime and beautiful Mr. Locke's doctrine is oppofed; and it is contended that words are independent of ideas. The author applied this doctrine only to works of tafte, but
particularly

particularly to poetry. But in the subject to which Mr. Malone has extended the theory nothing surely can be more ridiculous than the use of words without ideas; and until any thing of the sublime and beautiful be discovered in the prose of that gentleman, the good sense and taste of the world will condemn the use of words which are utterly destitute of a meaning; especially when they are employed on a subject of reasoning and demonstration. Would not the conduct of that judge be ludicrous as well as indecent, who on a criminal matter, should use the words traitor, murderer, or thief, in his address to the jury, concerning the evidence before them? So in the controversy upon the Shakespeare MSS it would have been better reasoning, as well as more candid hostility, to have proved the imposture before he proclaimed the impostor.

In reply to these charges against me, I shall lay before the public some striking documents, which will constitute a most irrefragable system

of

of evidence in my favor, and furnifh the beft
refutation of what has been alledged againft me.
I fhall firft repeat that which I have told the
world already, and then I fhall enter into the
ftatements, which corroborate and fortify what
I have hitherto afferted.

In the preface to my folio collection of
Shakfpeare MSS I ftated all the circumftances
relative to them, as minutely as my own knowledge of them and the delicacy of my fituation
permitted me. I fhall now repeat the affertion,
with no other addition than my folemn proteftation of its truth.

" It may be expected, that fomething fhould
" be faid by the editor, of the manner in which
" thefe papers came into his hands. He recei-
" ved them from his Son, Samuel William
" Henry Ireland, a young man, then under
" nineteen years of age, by whom the difco-
" very was accidentally made at the houfe of a
" gentleman of confiderable property."
" Amongft

" Amongſt a maſs of family papers, the
" contracts between Shakſpeare, Lowine and
" Condell, and the leaſe granted by him and
" Hemynge to Michael Fraſer, which was firſt
" found, were diſcovered, and ſoon after the
" deed of gift to William Henry Ireland (de-
" ſcribed as the friend of Shakſpeare, in con-
" ſequence of his having ſaved his life on the
" river Thames, when in extreme danger of
" being drowned) and aiſo the deed of truſt to
" John Hemynge were diſcovered. In purſu-
" ing this ſearch, he was ſo fortunate as to diſ-
" cover ſome deeds very material to the in-
" tereſts of this gentleman, and ſuch as eſta-
" bliſhed beyond all doubt, his title to a conſi-
" derable property. In return for this ſervice,
" added to the conſideration, that the young
" man bore the ſame name, and arms, with
" the perſon, who ſaved the life of Shakſpeare,
" the gentleman promiſed him every thing re-
" lative to the ſubject, that had been or ſhould
" be found either in town or at his country
" houſe. At this houſe the principal part of
" the

" the papers, with a great variety of books
" containing the MSS notes and three MSS
" plays, with part of another were difco-
" vered."

" Fortified as he is with the opinion of the
" unprejudiced and the intelligent, the editor
" will not allow that it can be prefumption in
" him to fay, that he has no doubt of the truth
" and authenticity of that which he lays before
" the public. Of this fact he is as fully fatis-
" fied, as he is with the honor that has been
" obferved to him upon this fubject. So cir-
" cumftanced, he fhould not feel juftified in im-
" portuning, or any way requefting a gentle-
" man, to whom he is known only by obliga-
" gation, to fubject himfelf to the impertinence
" and licentioufnefs of literary curiofity and ca-
" vil, unlefs he fhould himfelf voluntarily come
" forward. But this is not all. It was not till
" after the mafs of papers received, became vo-
" luminous, that Mr. Ireland had any idea of

B   " printing

" printing them : he then applied for his per-
" miffion fo to do,* and this was not obtained,
" but under the ftrongeft injunction that his
" name fhould not appear. This injunction
" has thro' all the ftages of this bufinefs been
" uniformly declared : and, as this gentleman
" has dealt moft liberally with the editor, he
" can confidently fay, that in his turn he has
" with equal opennefs and candour conducted
" himfelf towards the public, to whom imme-
" diately upon every communication made,
" every thing has been fubmitted without
" referve."

The information, which induced me to lay
this ftatement before the public, was derived
from written declarations of my fon, and from

* The reader is here requefted to underftand, that the
application made to the fuppofed original poffeffor, was not
perfonal, but by letters given by him to his fon, to be conveyed by him, and by anfwers received, thro' the fame
channel.

thofe

thofe of his friend Mr. Talbot, of the Dublin Theatre. I now prefent to the world the account of the difcovery, as it was written by my fon, and which is at this time, in my poffeffion.

" *November* 10th, 1795.

" I was at chambers, when Talbot called
" in, and fhewed me a deed, figned Shakfpeare.
" I was much aftonifhed, and mentioned the
" pleafure my father would receive, could he
" but fee it. Talbot then faid, I might fhew
" it. I did not for two days : and at the end
" of that term he gave it me. I then preffed
" hard to know, where it was found. After
" two or three days had elapfed, he introduced
" me to the party. He was with me in the
" room, but took little trouble in fearching.
" I found a fecond deed, and a third, and two
" or three loofe papers. We alfo difcovered
" a deed, which afcertained to the party landed
" property, of which he had then no knowledge.
" In confequence of having found this, he told

" us,

" us, we might keep every deed, every scrap
" of paper relative to Shakspeare. Little was
" discovered in town, but what was above men-
" tioned, but the rest came from the country;
" owing to the papers having been removed from
" London, many years ago.

" S. W. H. Ireland."

Being naturally desirous of obtaining the evidence of Mr. Talbot, to confirm what had been
advanced by my son, I applied to the former,
and received from him an answer, from which I
have made the following extracts.

Carmarthen, November 25, 1795.

" Dear Sir,

" The gentleman, in whose possession these
" things were found, was a friend of mine; and
" by me your Son Samuel was introduced to his
" acquaintance. One morning in rummaging
" from mere curiosity some old lumber, consist-
" ing of deeds, books, &c. in a closet of my
" friend's house, I discovered a deed with the
" signature

" fignature of William Shakfpeare, which in-
" duced me to read part of it, and on reading
" the words " Stratford on Avon" I was con-
" vinced it was the famous Englifh Bard: with
" permiffion of my friend (whom I will in future
" call Mr. H———) I carried the deed to Sa-
" muel, knowing with what enthufiafm, he and
" yourfelf regarded the works of that author,
" or any trifling article he was poffeffed of;
" though I was prepared to fee my friend Sa-
" muel a little pleafed with what I prefented to
" him, yet I did not expect that great joy he
" felt on the occafion. He told me there was
" nothing known of the hand writing of Shak-
" fpeare, but his fignature to fome deed or will
" in Doctors Commons, and preffed me to carry
" him to H———'s houfe, that he might fee,
" if there was amongft the lumber I had fpoken
" of, any other fuch relique. I immediately
" complied with his requeft. This was Samuel's
" firft introduction. For feveral fucceffive
" mornings we paffed fome hours in examining
" different papers and deeds, moft of which
.   " were

" were ufelefs, and uninterefting. But our
" labor was rewarded by finding a few more
" relating to Shakfpeare. Thefe we took away,
" but never without H's permiffion. At laft
" we were fo fortunate as to difcover a deed,
" in which our friend was materially concerned.
" Some landed property, which had been long
" the fubject of litigation was here afcertained,
" and H's title to it clearly proved. H. now
" faid in return for this, whatever you and Mr.
" Ireland find among the lumber, be it what it
" may, fhall be your own (meaning thofe things
" which we fhould prize for being Shakfpeare's)
" Mr. H. juft before my departure from Lon-
" don, ftrictly enjoined us never to mention him
" as the poffeffor of the papers. Tho' I wifhed
" until Sam. fhould have completed his re-
" fearches, that little fhould have been faid on
" the fubject, yet I was ignorant, why H. when
" the fearch was finifhed, fhould ftill wifh his
" name concealed. I thought it abfurd and
" could not prevail on him to mention his rea-
" fons; tho' from fome trifling unguarded ex-
" preffion

" pression, I was at last induced to believe that
" one of his anceftors was a cotemporary of
" Shakfpeare in the dramatic profeffion; that
" as he H. was a man fomewhat known in the
" world, and in the walk of high life, he did
" not wifh fuch a circumftance fhould be made
" public; this fufpicion was, as it will prefently
" appear, well founded. Whilft I was in Dub-
" lin, I heard to my great joy and aftonifhment,
" that Sam had difcovered the play of Vorti-
" gern and Rowena, the MS of Lear, &c.
" &c. I was impatient to hear every parti-
" cular, and principally for that purpofe made
" my late vifit to London. I found H. what I
" always thought him, a Man of ftrict honor,
" and willing to abide by the promife he made,
" in confequence of our finding the deed, by
" which he benefitted fo much. I will now ex-
" plain the reafon of H's fecrecy. On account
" of your defire to give the world fome explan-
" ation of the bufinefs, and your telling me,
" that fuch explanation was neceffary, I re-
" newed my entreaties to him, to fuffer us to dif-

" difcover

" cover his name, place of abode, and every
" circumftance of the difcovery of the papers,
" but in vain. I proceeded to prove as well
" as I could the folly of its concealment, when
" he produced a deed of gift, which he himfelf
" had juft found in the clofet, juft before my
" departure from London, in January laft, but
" which I had never feen before. By this deed
" William Shakfpeare affigned to John ———
" who it feems was really an anceftor of our friend
" H. every article contained in an upper room.
" The articles were, furniture, cups, a miniature
" picture, and many other things; but except-
" ing the miniature (which was lately found
" and which was a likenefs of Shakfpeare him-
" felf), and the papers, very few of them re-
" main in H's hands, and the reft very unfor-
" tunately cannot be traced. It is fuppofed too,
" that many valuable papers have been loft, and
" are deftroyed, as the whole lumber is never
" remembered to have been at all valued or
" guarded from the hands of the loweft domef-
" tics. When I parted from you a few weeks

fince

" since, H. promised me that the deed of
" gift above mentioned should be sent you,
" first erasing and cutting out the name of the
" grantee.* I hope, my dear Sir, I have omit-
" ted nothing in relating these circumstances;
" and though this account may not enable you
" perfectly to satisfy many, who from an idle
" curiosity would know more, yet the liberal-
" minded, I am sure will allow that you have
" just reasons for with-holding what is, and is to
" be concealed. I most earnestly beg you will
" send me a copy of Vortigern and Rowena, as
" soon as it can conveniently be written, with the
" margin marked, according to the curtailment
" for Stage representation.

" M. Talbot.

" S. Ireland, Esq."

* Within a few days after the receipt of the above, the
deed of trust alluded to, was brought to me by my Son,
without any erasure, as mentioned in the above letter, and
was the deed of trust to John Hemynge, inserted in the folio
volume of the Shakspeare papers.

C

Upon

Upon this authority and with this degree of testimony, I proceeded to the publication of the papers. - Yet it may by some be objected, that the weight of the whole evidence collectively taken, is still weak and imperfect, on account of the concealment of the name of the gentleman alluded to. But what inference does this objection authorise? It was such as entirely to militate against any suspicion of fraud in my breast. For had the papers been forged, I could not imagine that the fabricators of it would have left that part of its evidence, to which by ordinary minds, and according to ordinary rules of judgment, the greatest weight is usually attributed, so palpably mutilated, and defective. I could not imagine that it could have been the work of one impostor, when I considered the infinite variety of the papers, and the length of time which must have been consumed on so elaborate a fiction. For it must have been very extraordinary, that of all those who were concerned in the imposture, not one should have

suggested

suggested the necessity of forging completer testimonies, respecting the place, and person, in whose possession they were found.

Besides these reasons, coming as they did through the channel of my Son, I could not suspect their authenticity; and every thing I had remarked of Mr. Talbot during my acquaintance with him, placed him in my judgment beyond even the possibility of suspicion, his fairness and honesty in the transaction appeared invariable. A father is not very eager to entertain surmises, that affect the moral credit of one so dearly connected with him as his only son, and when the same declarations were made by him in the most solemn and awful manner, before crowds of the most eminent characters, who came to my house, I could not suffer myself to cherish the slightest suspicion of his veracity.

The testimonies here adduced it were difficult to resist. But these were not all by which my conduct was governed in this transaction.

I in-

I invited to my house all who wished to gratify their curiosity, by an inspection of the papers. Of these, the greater part consisting of the most celebrated literary characters this age has produced, expressed their opinions, not in the phrase of mere assent, but in the unequivocal language of a full and overflowing conviction. Some were even desirous of subscribing without solicitation, their names to a certificate, in which their belief might be formally and permanently recorded. The first of this respectable list was the rev. Dr. Parr. I informed this gentleman, that the late James Boswell, Esq. had requested my permission to annex his name to a certificate, vouching for the validity of the papers and which he drew up for that purpose. When I shewed the Doctor, at his request what Mr. Boswell had written the day before, he exclaimed with his characteristic energy and manner, that it was too feebly expressed for the importance of the subject; and begged that he might himself dictate to me the following form of a certificate, to which he immediately subscribed his own name,

and which afterwards received the signatures of
the other respectable characters, that are annexed to it.

    " We whose names are hereunto subscribed
" have, in the presence and by the favor of
" Mr. Ireland, inspected the Shakspeare papers,
" and are convinced of their authenticity."

        Samuel Parr.
        John Tweddell.
        Thomas Burgess.
        John Byng.
        James Bindley.
        Herbert Croft.
        Somerset.
        If. Heard, Garter King of Arms.
        F. Webb.
        R. Valpy.
        James Boswell.*

   * Mr. Boswell, previous to figning his name, fell upon
his knees, and in a tone of enthufiafm, and exultation,
thanked God, that he had lived to witnefs this difcovery,
and exclaimed that he could now die in peace.

                       Lauderdale.

Lauderdale.

Rev. J. Scott.

Kinnaird.

John Pinkerton.

Thomas Hunt.

Henry James Pye.

Rev. N. Thornbury.

Jonⁿ. Hewlett, Tranſlator of old Records, Common Pleas Office, Temple.

Mat. Wyatt.

John Frank Newton.

The following is a catalogue of the papers above alluded to, dated

February 25th, 1795.

1. Viz. Shakſpeare's profeſſion of faith on two ſmall ſheets of paper.

2. His copy of a letter to Lord Southampton, and Lord Southampton's anſwer.

3. His letter to Richard Cowley, incloſing a curious drawing in pen and ink of himſelf.

4. His

4. His letter to Anna Hatherwaye, the lady whom he afterwards married, inclosing a braided lock of his hair.

5. Five poetical ftanzas, addreffed to the fame lady, in his own hand writing.

6. His note of hand, payable one month after date to John Hemynge, for five pounds, and five fhillings, together with John Hemynge's receipt the day it became due.

7. A leafe of fix acres of land, and two houfes abutting on the Globe Theatre, granted by William Shakfpeare to Michael Frafer, and. figned and fealed by the refpective parties.

8. Deed of agreement between William Shakfpeare and Henry Condell for the weekly payment of a certain fum therein fpecified for the theatrical fervices of the faid Henry Condell, figned and fealed by the refpective parties.

9. Deed

9. Deed of agreement between William Shakſpeare and John Lowine for the weekly payment of a certain ſum therein ſpecified for the theatrical ſervices of the ſaid John Lowine, ſigned and ſealed by the reſpective parties.

10. A ſmall whole length of a tinted drawing, ſuppoſed to be of Shakſpeare in the character of Baſſanio, and on the reverſe ſide the whole length of a perſon in the character of Shylock, in its original black frame.

11. An original letter of Queen Elizabeth to Shakſpeare, authenticated by himſelf.

In *March* 1796, In conſequence of Mr. Albany Wallis having recently made a diſcovery of ſome deeds relative to Shakeſpeare and Ireland, the following Certificate was ſigned by the gentlemen, whoſe names are annexed to it, after having carefully peruſed and collated the ſaid deeds with thoſe in my poſſeſſion.

" *London,*

" *London, March,* 1796.

" We the underfigned, having infpected the
" following deeds in the poffeffion of Albany
" Wallis, Efq. of Norfolk Street, viz.

" A conveyance, dated 10th *March,* 1612,
" faid to be from Henry Walker to William
" Shakfpeare, William Johnfon, John Jackfon,
" and John Hemynges, of a houfe in Black-
" friars, then or late being in the occupation of
" one William Ireland; figned Wm. Shak-
" fpeare, Jo. Jackfon, and Wm. Johnfon.

" And a deed dated 10th *February,* 1617,
" being a conveyance figned Jo. Jackfon, Wm.
" Johnfon, and John Hemynges of the fame
" premifes;

" Having alfo infpected the following papers
" of Mr. Samuel Ireland of Norfolk Street,
" viz.

D   " A MS.

" A MS. Play of Lear, a fragment of
" Hamlet, a play of Vortigern—feveral deeds,
" witnefled Wm. Shakfpeare—feveral receipts
" and notes of difburfements of monies on ac-
" count of the Globe and certain Theatres—
" familiar letters figned Wm. Shakfpeare, and
" other mifcellaneous MSS.

" And having compared the hand writing of
" the above papers in Mr. Ireland's poffeffion,
" with the fignatures of Shakfpeare and He-
" mynge to the deed in Mr. Wallis's hands, as
" well as with the publifhed Fac-fimiles of the
" autographs of Shakfpeare to his laft will and
" teftament, and to a deed dated 11 *March*, 10
" Jac. I. which came to the hands of Mr. Wal-
" lis, about the year 1760, among the title deeds
" of the Rev. Mr. Fetherftonehaugh, and from
" the character and manner thereof, we declare
" our firm belief in the authenticity of the auto-
" graphs of Shakfpeare, and Hemynge, in the
" hands of Mr. Ireland.

Ifaac

Ifaac Heard, Gr. K. at Arms.

Francis Webb.

Albany Wallis.

Richard Troward.

Jonⁿ. Hewlett, Tranflator of old Records,
    Common Pleas Office, Temple.

John Byng.

Francis Townfend, Windfor Herald.

Gilbert Franklin, Wimpole Street.

Matthew Wyatt, New Inn.

Richard Valpy, Reading.

Jofeph Skinner.

Frank Newton, Wimpole Street.

It may perhaps be almoft unneceffary to ftate that I might have obtained innumerable fignatures to each of the certificates, I have laid before the public, had I reforted to any folicitations for the purpofe. The very refpectable lift of fubfcribers to the publication of Shakfpeare's MSS may be adverted to, as a corroborating proof in favor of their validity and in juftification of my fending them into the world.

D 2   I fhall

I shall now present to the reader a voluntary deposition formally drawn on stamped paper, and intended to be taken before a magistrate by my son.

" Samuel William Henry Ireland, of Nor-
" folk Street, in the parish of St. Clement
" Danes, in the county of Middlesex, Gent,
" maketh voluntary oath that since the 16th day
" of Dec. 1794, he this deponent hath at various
" times deposited in the house of this deponent's
" Father, Samuel Ireland, of Norfolk Street
" aforesaid, several deeds and MSS papers
" signed and supposed to be written by Wm.
" Shakspear and others. And this deponent
" farther maketh oath and faith that the deeds
" and MSS papers now open for inspection,
" at his this deponent's father's house, are the
" same which he this deponent so deposited as
" aforesaid ; and whereas several disputes have
" arisen concerning the originality of the deeds
" and MS papers aforesaid, and whereas Ed-
" mond Malone, of Queen Anne Street East, of
" the

" the parish of St. Mary-le-Bone, in the said
" county of Middlesex, hath publickly adver-
" vertised or caused to be advertised an assertion
" to the effect that he, the said Edmond Ma-
" lone, had discovered the above mentioned
" papers and MS deeds to be a forgery, which
" assertion may tend to injure the reputation of
" his the said deponent's father. Now this de-
" ponent farther maketh oath that he this de-
" ponent's father, the said Samuel Ireland, hath
" not, nor hath any one of the said Samuel Ire-
" land's family, other than save and except this
" deponent, any knowledge of the manner in
" which he the said deponent, became possessed
" of the said deeds or MSS papers aforesaid or
" any part thereof, or of any circumstance, or
" circumstances relating thereto,

" S. W. H. Ireland.

" Sworn before me this   day of March,
" 1796."

Copied verbatim from the hand writing of
my Son.

It

It being thought unneceſſary to enter into
a formal depoſition upon the ſubject, my ſon was
not ſworn to what he has here depoſed. But
Mr. Albany Wallis in May following drew
up the advertiſement which I have here ſub-
joined, conceiving it more adequate to the pur-
poſe, which was inſerted in the True Briton,
Morning Herald, and other papers.

" Shakſpeare MSS,

" In juſtice to my father, and to remove
" the reproach, under which he has innocently
" fallen, reſpecting the papers publiſhed by him
" as the MSS of Shakſpeare, I do hereby
" ſolemnly declare that they were given to him
" by me, as the genuine productions of Shakſ-
" peare, and that he was and is at this moment
" totally unacquainted with the ſource from
" whence they came, or with any circumſtance
" concerning them, ſave what he was told by
" myſelf, and which he has declared in the
" preface to his publication. With this firm
" belief

" belief and conviction of their authenticity,
" founded on the credit he gave to me and my
" affurances, they were laid before the world.
" This will be further confirmed, when at some
" future period it may be judged expedient to
" difclose the means by which they were ob-
" tained.

" S. W. H. Ireland, Jun."

Witnefs,

Albany Wallis.

Thomas Trowfdale, Clerk to Meffrs.

   Wallis and Troward.

Norfolk Street, May 24, 1796.

This is furely very ample teftimony, which
my fon has adduced, to eftablifh my innocence
of the imputed forgery. I corroborate this teftimony by fome further quotations from feveral
letters, written by Mr. M. Talbot, already
mentioned to myfelf and my family, of which
the originals are preferved in my poffeffion.

Dublin,

Dublin, 15th *April,* 1796.

" So much do I lament the unfortunate
" predicament in which Mr. Ireland is involv-
" ed, that I muſt do every thing in my power
" to extricate him from it, conſiſtent with my
" own honour, and oath. The offer I ſhall
" make, therefore will, I hope, be accepted
" definitively without urging any more propoſals,
" ſince any others muſt of neceſſity be declined
" by me, though my life were the forfeit for
" being ſecret. I will make an affidavit jointly
" with Sam. " *That Mr. Ireland is innocent of any*
" *forgery imputed to him; that he is equally as unac-*
" *quainted with the diſcovery of the papers, as the*
" *world in general; that he has been only the pub-*
" *liſher of them: aud that the ſecret is known to*
" *no more than Sam. myſelf, and a third perſon,*
" *whom Mr. Ireland is not acquainted with.*"

" If

" If our making this affidavit and the pub-
" lication of it will ferve Mr. Ireland, Sam
" and myfelf are both ready to ftand forward."

" If I may venture an opinion, I ftill think
" it probable that the papers are genuine, that
" Vortigern may have been one of Shakfpeare's
" firft effays at dramatic writing."

" The play of Henry 2d I never have feen,
" nor the manufcript of Vortigern, nor any
" thing relative to it, till I was in London, long
" after the latter was in Mr. Sheridan's hands.
" I muft therefore depend on the veracity of
" others, as to their coming from the fame
" fource as the few manufcripts I faw before I
" left London the firft time."

" Mr. Ireland has defired my opinion re-
" fpecting a plan he propofes of making two
" gentlemen of refpectability acquainted with
" every circumftance, who are to vouch to the
" world for the authenticity of the MSS.

E   " This

" 'This will not be confiftent with our promife
" and oath."

" M. Talbot."

It is worth remarking, that about a week
before the receipt of this letter (and ftrange as
it may appear, at the particular requeft of my
fon) a committee confifting of twenty-four refpectable gentlemen met at my houfe, for the
purpofe of taking into confideration every circumftance relative to the MSS and the obloquy
under which I laboured, in confequence of their
publication. This committee met at three different times within the month of April, and my
fon was prefent at each of their meetings; at
which he propofed that two refpectable perfons
who were not members of the committee, fhould
be appointed to receive the following information.

" The gentlemen are to be informed
" whence the papers came, the name of the
" gentleman, to whom they belonged, by whom
" difcovered,

" difcovered, and in what place, and manner.
" The fchedule of thofe that remain behind is
" in my father's poffeffion, which he may fhew,
" and which fhall be accounted for by me."

" S. W. H. Ireland."

Copied verbatim from the above paper in
his own hand writing, and in his prefence read
to the Committee.

It muft be obvious that this propofal does
not concur with Mr. Talbot's opinion, as quoted
from his letter above.

The following fchedule, likewife, was prefented to the committee by my fon, accompa-
nied with a folemn proteftation, that every article
marked with * he had feen, and would in a fhort
time be put into my hands : that thofe, which

had

had not this mark, he had only heard were in existence, but that he had not seen them.*

* Play of Richard II. in Shakspeare's MS.
* Play of Henry II.
* ——— of Henry V.
* 62 leaves of K. John.
* 49 leaves of Othello.
* 37 leaves of Richard III.
* 37 leaves of Timon of Athens.
* 14 leaves of Henry IV.
* 7 leaves of Julius Cæsar.
* Catalogue of his books in his own MS.
* Deed by which he became partner of the Curtain Theatre, with Benjamin Kele, and John Hemynges.
* Two drawings of the Globe Theatre on parchment.
* Verses to Q. Elizabeth.

* This schedule was voluntarily written by my son, on the 10th Jan. 1796, in the presence of Geo. Chalmers, and J. Reeves, Esqrs.

* Verses

* Verfes to Sir Francis Drake.
* Do. to Sir Walter Raleigh.
* Miniature of Shakfpeare fet in filver,
Chaucer with his MS notes
Book relative to Q. Elizabeth do.
Euphues with do.
Bible with do.
Bochas's Works with his MS notes.
Barclay's Ship of Fools do.
Hollinfhed's Chronicle do.
Brief account of his life in his own hand,
Whole length portrait, faid to be of him in
    oil,

The committees alluded to, met three times
without arriving at any fatisfactory determina-
tions; and as we found it difficult to felect two
perfons to receive the information, my fon had
promifed, Mr. Albany Wallis, as a profeffional
man, voluntarily offered to be himfelf the depofi-
tary of the fecret. This truft, as he fays, he was
induced to accept, in order to clear up any doubt
in the mind of the fuppofed Gentleman as to
              any

any part of his property that might be endangered by such disclosure. In consequence of this, my son had frequent interviews with Mr. Wallis. But what was communicated, at those conferences, I have not learned from that gentleman, notwithstanding my reiterated importunities, and most anxious solicitations for that purpose. His uniform answer to these solicitations was, " Do not ask me any questions. It is not proper that you should know the secret. Keep " your mind easy; all will be well in time."

In support of these testimonies, by which my innocence must be clearly established in the judgments of all, who have the slightest pretensions to candor, or found sense, I will make another quotation from a letter I received from Mr. Talbot, dated Cork, Sept. 16th, 1796,

" Dear Sir,

" Your last letter to me should have been " answered sooner, and the promised affidavit
" been

" been sent, if I could have obtained an answer
" from your Son to something I wrote about
" some time since. For without his consenting,
" if not joining in such a proceeding, I did
" not think myself authorised, in taking any
" step whatever."

" I will do all I can to extricate you from
" any difficulties you may labour under, and
" not having heard any thing from your son,
" I will make an affidavit solely, That from
" my intimacy with him, and my own know-
" ledge of the mystery of the MSS you were
" innocent of any design to mislead or deceive
" the public."

" I beg leave to assure you, that I shall feel
" the greatest pleasure in standing forward to
" screen you, who are an innocent sufferer."

" M. Talbot."

I have now exhibited to the world all the
testimonies of which I am in possession, relative
to

to the difcovery of thefe papers. Whatever impreffion they are likely to produce, with regard to their authenticity, or fpurioufnefs, they who can doubt my innocence in the tranfactions, after this ftatement muft be hardened with an incurable malice, or an impenetrable incredulity. Yet for nearly two years, I have been expofed to the animadverfions of every half-formed, and puny critic, who has been fo far initiated in the elements of language, as to compofe a malicious paragraph, and imbibed fo much of the fpirit of his fraternity, as to miftake petulance and flander for reafon and inveftigation.

Befides thefe evils, I have reafon to complain of the low tricks, and artifices, that have been reforted to, in order to excite the public prejudice againft the MSS. I allude to the fteps that were taken to preclude the Play of Vortigern from an equitable, and candid hearing. In fupport of this affertion, let me refer the reader to the following advertifement, publifhed

lifhed by Mr. Malone, nearly three months before his enquiry made its appearance.

" Spurious Shakfpeare MSS.
" Mr. Malone's detection of this forgery
" has been unavoidably delayed by the engrav-
" ings having taken more time than was ex-
" pected ; but it is hoped that it will be ready
" by the end of this month.
" *Feb.* 16, 1796."

With regard to the delay, which the author
of the advertifement feems to lament, I am
compelled from my own knowledge of engrav-
ing, to conclude that it was wholly intentional.
I know, and I fpeak with confidence on the
fubject, that with very little diligence the en-
gravings, which Mr. Malone has incorrectly
copied from my publication, would require a
very fmall portion of time, for their completion.
On the 25th of March, however, the play having been already advertifed for the 2d of April,
we find the critic, and his fellow labourers the
engravers in fuch a ftate of forwardnefs that the

F   publication

publication was advertised for Thursday March 31st, only two days before the intended representation of the piece. That it might be absolutely impossible that the mischief should not take effect, in several papers of the 1st of April, particularly the Oracle, and Morning Herald, two different and elaborate critiques in praise of Mr. Malone's enquiry made their appearance.

No man can entertain a doubt concerning the purposes, this well constructed delay was meant to answer. The play was ready for representation. It was to make its appeal to the general judgment ; and to stand or fall by its decision. But it was the scheme of this critic, to intercept this appeal; to choak, and obstruct the avenues to the public understanding, and to overwhelm it with a torrent of ill-founded prejudices, and anticipated convictions.

I cannot pass over this part of the subject, without remarking, that in order to counteract as much as possible, the mischief of these artifices;

fices, I inferted three days afterwards an advertifement in the papers, in which I animadverted
in very fevere terms on the temerity of characterifing his work, as a detection. In reply to
this, Mr. Malone inferts a letter in the Gentleman's Magazine, in which he vindicates himfelf from the charge, in the following words.
" With refpect to the literary temerity afcribed
" to him (Mr. Malone) in characterifing his
" work as a detection, he has no apprehenfion,
" that he fhall incur any cenfure from the judi-
" cious part of mankind, fince in this point of
" view he only benches by the fide of his learned
" friend the prefent very refpectable Lord Bi-
" fhop of Salifbury, who 46 years ago publifhed
" a defervedly admired tract, on a fimilar fub-
" ject, thus intitled, Milton no Plagiary, or a
" Detection of the forgeries contained in Lau-
" der's Effay, on the imitation of the moderns
" in the Paradife Loft by Milton. By the rev.
" John Douglas, &c."

I have made this quotation, that the world

may

may remark the indecent effrontery of drawing an analogy between the rev. Bifhop, and the author of the enquiry. Not to mention the wide and unmeafurable diftance, between the literary endowments of the two writers, it muft be palpable to every one, that there is no refemblance at all between the circumftances of Lauder's forgery, and the difcovery of the MSS in my poffeffion.

It is now time for me to clofe this part of the fubject. I have fhewn that the manner in which the artifices, of which I complain, have been conducted, is of fo mean and pufillanimous a nature, that the malice has been of fo low and fo contemptible a fpecies, as to reflect very ferious difhonour on him, who has condefcended to make ufe of it, becaufe it may naturally be imagined, that a perfon calling himfelf a fcholar and a gentleman, might have had recourfe to worthier and more dignified weapons of controverfy.

The other part of this work will be allotted

to

to an inveſtigation of the critical attacks, that
have been directed againſt the papers, in which
I truſt that Mr. Malone will be completely refuted. Perhaps it might be expected of me,
that I ſhould advert to the other antagoniſts,
who have appeared in the field of the controverſy. Of the firſt of theſe publications, entitled " A Letter to George Steevens, Eſq. con-
" taining a Critical examination, &c. &c," As
it has been abundantly refuted in a very able
pamphlet, entitled " A Comparative Review of
" the opinion, &c. &c." I ſhall ſay nothing further. One Waldron likewiſe, has waded into the
controverſy, a bad actor and a worſe critic. Theſe
are men, on whom I ſhall not animadvert. They
who miſtake their vanity for their capacity,
and ſuppoſe that they are qualified to perform
what they have preſumption to attempt, are a
tribe, on whom admonition will be waſted, and
rebuke will be ſuperfluous.

But I have confined my reaſoning to Mr.
Malone ; becauſe, as he is known to the world
by

by what may be emphatically called his literary *labours* on other occasions, so has he distinguish- ed himself by the bulk of his criticisms on this. What Dr. Warburton said of poor Theobald, he would have said with infinitely more justice of this critic : " That what he read he could " transcribe ; but as what he thought, if " ever he did think, he could but ill express, " so he read on ; and by that means got a cha- " racter of learning, without risquing the im- " putation of wanting a better talent." In the part, however, which he has taken in this con- troversy, he has brought the only literary qua- lity he has, that of patient, and laborious re- search, into suspicion. Whether it be the in- stinctive property of dulness to be dark, and bewildered, in proportion to the efforts it makes to be bright and perspicuous, or that though he has much reading, he has not enough for the office he has arrogated, it is certain that his book abounds with so many blunders, and overflows with so much presumption, that it seems a sort of mixed animal, engendered between

tween a perfevering dulnefs on one fide, and an envious mind on the other.

If I fucceed in proving what I have afferted, I fhall do a very effential fervice to literature itfelf. I. fhall have ridded the literary world of a fort of ufurper. I fhall have pulled from his dictatorfhip a man, who has afpired with the moft prefumptuous arrogance to a kind of oracular dignity on thefe matters. I fhall have refcued the underftandings of the public from the dominion of a critic, who, relying on the bulk of his labours, and the ponderous mafs of his refearches, has attempted to give laws on all topics of literature and criticifm.

But, fhould I not effect this purpofe, I fhall at leaft retire from the public tribunal with the foothing confcioufnefs, of having vindicated my own character. For I truft I have laid before the world, a mafs of documents, which will effectually lift me above the ftroke of the venomous afperfions that have been directed fo perfeveringly againft me. Should the language I

have

have occafionally ufed in thefe attacks, appear
harfh and irritable, I beg to obferve in my juftification, that Mr. Malone's ftrictures are
uniformly clothed in the language of afperity
and perfonal farcafm; and furely fome indul-
gence ought to be allowed me, if I repel his attacks with the fame weapons, and reply to un-
juft infinuations in the diction of indignant and
wounded feelings. It was for the purpofe principally of vindicating myfelf that I have ven-
tured to make this appeal to the public. I
might indeed complain of other misfortunes.
I might advert to the pecuniary loffes and the
confumption of time, which thefe tranfactions
have led me into. But when the moft valuable
of all human benefits, a clear and unfullied
character is endangered, I could not but look
on every other evil, as of trivial and fubor-
dinate confideration.

Norfolk Street,
November, 1796.

F I N I S.

www.ingramcontent.com/pod-product-compliance
Lightning Source LLC
Chambersburg PA
CBHW030902260626
47169CB00008B/2653